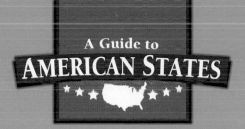
A Guide to
AMERICAN STATES

Rhode Island

THE OCEAN STATE

MEDIA ENHANCED BOOKS
AV2 BY WEIGL
ADDED VALUE • AUDIO VISUAL

www.av2books.com

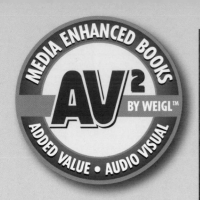

MEDIA ENHANCED BOOKS
AV2 BY WEIGL
ADDED VALUE · AUDIO VISUAL

Go to **www.av2books.com**, and enter this book's unique code.

BOOK CODE

R 1 4 5 4 5 6

AV² by Weigl brings you media enhanced books that support active learning.

AV² provides enriched content that supplements and complements this book. Weigl's AV² books strive to create inspired learning and engage young minds in a total learning experience.

Your AV² Media Enhanced books come alive with...

Audio
Listen to sections of the book read aloud.

Key Words
Study vocabulary, and complete a matching word activity.

Video
Watch informative video clips.

Quizzes
Test your knowledge.

Embedded Weblinks
Gain additional information for research.

Slide Show
View images and captions, and prepare a presentation.

Try This!
Complete activities and hands-on experiments.

... and much, much more!

Published by AV² by Weigl
350 5th Avenue, 59th Floor
New York, NY 10118
Website: www.av2books.com   www.weigl.com

Library of Congress Cataloging-in-Publication Data

Winans, Jay D.
 Rhode Island / Jay D. Winans.
    p. cm. -- (A guide to American states)
 Includes index.
 ISBN 978-1-61690-812-6 (hardcover : alk. paper) -- ISBN 978-1-61690-488-3 (online)
 1. Rhode Island--Juvenile literature. I. Title.
 F79.3.W563 2011
 974.5--dc23
                    2011019027

Printed in the United States of America in North Mankato, Minnesota

052011
WEP180511

Project Coordinator Jordan McGill
Art Director Terry Paulhus

Photo Credits
Every reasonable effort has been made to trace ownership and to obtain permission to reprint copyright material. The publishers would be pleased to have any errors or omissions brought to their attention so that they may be corrected in subsequent printings.

Weigl acknowledges Getty Images as its primary image supplier for this title.

Contents

Rhode Island's long coastline makes it easily accessible by boat or ferry.
Newport is a popular port for oceangoing vessels.

Introduction

R hode Island is the smallest state in the United States, covering only about 1,045 square miles of land. But it is not difficult to see that this state is brimming with industry, history, and culture. When the state's bays and islands are included, the coastline measures more than 400 miles. With this in mind, it should come as no surprise that the state's official nickname is the Ocean State. The Atlantic Ocean, the second-largest ocean in the world, has greatly influenced the state's economy and its people. The coast is the most important commercial area, supporting a vibrant fishing industry. And the call of the coast has attracted many visitors, making tourism yet another important economic activity in the state.

The Jamestown Windmill on Conanicut Island was built in 1787. It replaced a windmill destroyed during the American Revolution.

The Independent Man, a gold-covered bronze statue on top of the state house in Providence, is a symbol of freedom in Rhode Island.

Rhode Island is known for its independent nature. The state was founded in 1636 by Roger Williams after he was banished from a colony in Plymouth, Massachusetts, for his religious views. Williams and others established a settlement nearby and called it Providence. They welcomed people whose religious beliefs were not **tolerated** by the other colonies.

During the American Revolution, Rhode Island was the first state to declare independence. Rhode Island displayed its independent spirit again by being the last of the original 13 colonies to **ratify** the U.S. Constitution. Before giving its approval, Rhode Island demanded the addition of the Bill of Rights, which guarantees individual liberties.

Where Is Rhode Island?

Rhode Island is one of the New England states, along with Maine, New Hampshire, Vermont, Massachusetts, and Connecticut. Rhode Island's boundaries were not decided for many years after the American Revolution. The western boundary with Connecticut was not established until 1887. The northern and eastern boundaries with Massachusetts were finally settled in 1883 and 1899, respectively.

Rhode Island, close to several New England cities, draws many tourists to its beautiful natural areas, including Narragansett Bay.

Rhode Island prospered throughout the 1800s and attracted some of the country's wealthiest citizens. Many went to the state to take advantage of the commercial opportunities in the Narragansett Bay area. Today the economy enjoys modest growth based on wholesale and retail sales, real estate, and tourism. Manufacturing, especially of silverware, jewelry, and electronic products, also contributes to the economy. Agriculture and fishing remain valued traditional industries in Rhode Island.

Travelers can get to Rhode Island by land, sea, or air. Interstate Highways 95 and 295 are the main roadways from Connecticut and Massachusetts. Numerous train lines serve the state, including Amtrak for passenger travel. Rhode Island's main airport is T.F. Green International Airport in Warwick. Conveniently located within a short drive of Boston, Cape Cod, Newport, and Providence, this airport serves many New England travelers.

T.F. Green International Airport in Warwick was the first state-owned airport in the United States.

Mapping Rhode Island

Rhode Island shares a border with two other New England states. Connecticut lies to the west, and Massachusetts is to the north and east. Rhode Island's southwest corner shares a water border with New York. This border runs through the eastern end of Long Island Sound. The rest of the state borders the waters of Narragansett Bay and Rhode Island Sound.

Sites and Symbols

STATE SEAL
Rhode Island

STATE BIRD
Rhode Island Red

STATE FLOWER
Violet

STATE FLAG
Rhode Island

STATE FISH
Striped Bass

STATE TREE
Red Maple

Nickname The Ocean State

Motto Hope

Song "Rhode Island's It for Me," words by Charlie Hall and music by Maria Day

Entered the Union May 29, 1790, as the 13th state

Capital Providence

Population (2010 Census) 1,052,567

Ranked 43rd state

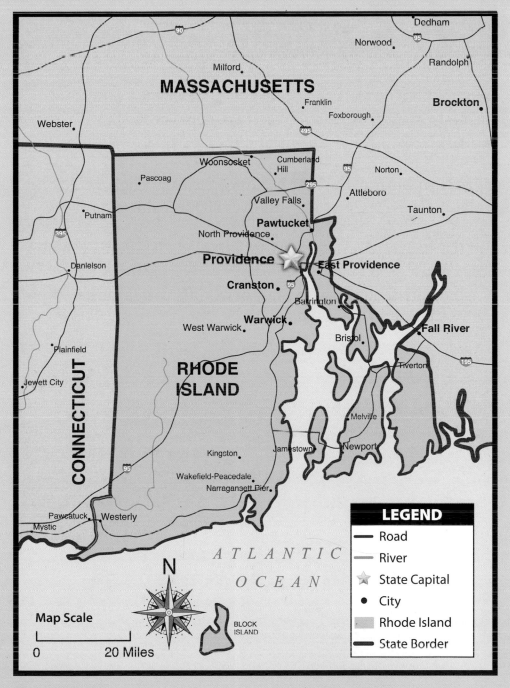

MASSACHUSETTS

Dedham
Norwood
Randolph
Milford
Franklin
Foxborough
Brockton
Webster
Norton
Cumberland Hill
Woonsocket
Pascoag
Attleboro
Valley Falls
Taunton
Putnam
Pawtucket
North Providence
Danielson
Providence
East Providence
Cranston
Barrington
Warwick
Fall River
West Warwick
Bristol
Tiverton
Plainfield
RHODE ISLAND
Jewett City
Melville
Kingston
Jamestown
Newport
Wakefield-Peacedale
Narragansett Pier
Pawcatuck
Westerly
Mystic

ATLANTIC OCEAN

N

CONNECTICUT

Map Scale

0   20 Miles

BLOCK ISLAND

LEGEND
— Road
— River
⭐ State Capital
• City
▢ Rhode Island
— State Border

STATE CAPITAL

The capital of Rhode Island is Providence. Located at the northern end of Narragansett Bay, Providence was incorporated as a city in 1831. Newport shared the role of state capital with Providence from 1854 to 1900, when Providence became the sole state capital.

United States

Hawai'i   Alaska

Rhode Island

The Land

Despite Rhode Island's small area, the state offers a variety of landscapes. Rhode Island has two main land regions. They are the New England Upland and the Coastal Lowlands.

The western two-thirds of the state is part of the New England Upland. This hilly landscape has elevations just over 800 feet above sea level.

The rest of the state is part of the Coastal Lowlands. This area contains the coastline and a grouping of small islands in Narragansett Bay. Along the shore are sandy beaches and rocky cliffs. Narragansett Bay cuts about 28 miles into the mainland.

NARRAGANSETT BAY

Narragansett Bay is an inlet of the Atlantic Ocean. The bay is where Rhode Island's main rivers empty. The Providence, Sakonnet, and Seekonk rivers are really arms of Narragansett Bay, making them saltwater rivers.

SAPOWET MARSH

Sapowet Marsh Wildlife Preserve in Tiverton is located in the eastern area of the state. Salt ponds, tidal creeks, and reeds cover this part of Rhode Island.

SAND DUNES

The Coastal Lowlands include many sand dunes and beach areas, such as Watch Hill in Westerly, near the Connecticut border. Signs there remind people to stay on trails to protect the hills or mounds of sand that have been piled up by the wind.

ISLANDS

The state has 36 islands, which are part of the Coastal Lowlands. The largest island in Narragansett Bay is called Rhode or Aquidneck Island. Outside the bay is Block Island.

When major rainstorms hit Rhode Island,
rivers overflow and flood streets.

Climate

T he climate in Rhode Island is mild and humid. The average temperature is 29° Fahrenheit in January and 71° F in July. The state's highest recorded temperature was 104° F in Providence on August 2, 1975. Its lowest temperature, recorded in Greene on February 5, 1996, was –25° F.

The weather in the Ocean State is windy and, at times, unpredictable. Tropical storms can hit the state in the summer and blizzards in the winter. But after a severe storm strikes, the weather can sometimes turn quite calm in a matter of hours. Rhode Island receives an average of 42 inches of precipitation every year.

Average Annual Precipitation Across Rhode Island

Precipitation varies across even a small state like Rhode Island. What factors might explain why North Foster gets so much more rainfall than Block Island?

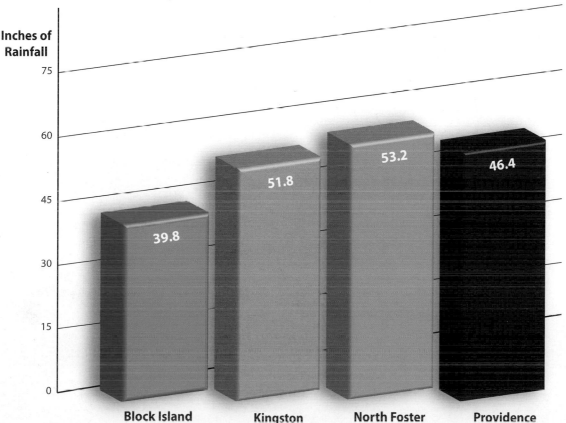

Natural Resources

Rhode Island has few large mineral deposits, but the land has something else to offer. The state has valuable soil. The soil in the western part of the state is rocky, while the soil in the eastern part near the ocean is sandy. The soil in the lowlands and on the islands is generally the best for cultivation. The richest soil is found near Narragansett Bay. There the soil is firm and not easily **eroded**. It is ideal for growing crops.

Narragansett Bay itself is an important natural resource. Running almost the length of the state's coastline, this large natural inlet has made it easier for Rhode Islanders to transport goods into and out of the state by ship. Rhode Island's fishing industry also depends on this coastal area.

Farmland in Rhode Island totals almost 68,000 acres.

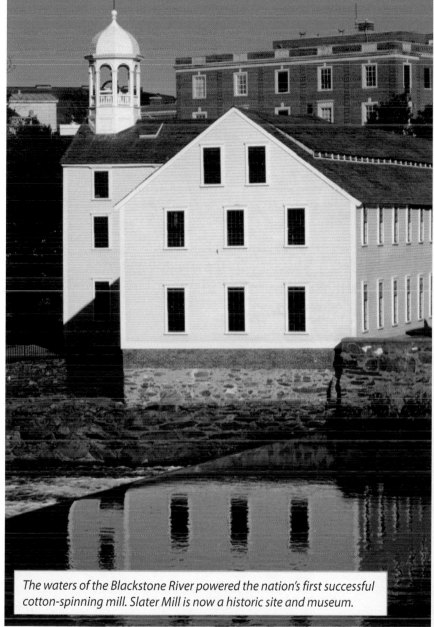

The waters of the Blackstone River powered the nation's first successful cotton-spinning mill. Slater Mill is now a historic site and museum.

Numerous rivers have also had a role in Rhode Island's economic success. The Blackstone, Pawtuxet, and Pawcatuck rivers provide fresh water and **hydroelectric** power to the people of Rhode Island.

Although mining is not a large industry in the state, it is part of the state's economy. Granite is the main mineral product of Rhode Island. This mineral, which is found in the southwest, is used as a building material.

Plants

Approximately 60 percent of the state is forested. Forests in Rhode Island consist of maples, oaks, ashes, birches, cedars, elms, and willows. Paper birches, which are also called canoe birches, thrive in the northernmost part of the state. American Indians peeled off the bark of these birches in long strips to make birchbark canoes.

In the marshlands near Charlestown, asters and cattails bloom. Dogwoods, mountain laurels, rhododendrons, trilliums, and violets grow in the woodlands. Seaweed grows in Rhode Island's coastal waters. It anchors to the ocean floor with rootlike ends. Unlike many plants, seaweed does not take in nutrients through its roots.

ASH TREE

Ash trees grow to about 50 feet in height. The wood of an ash tree is both strong and elastic.

FLOWERING DOGWOOD TREE

The flowering dogwood, native to eastern North America, is a small, bushy tree with small flowers. It usually grows no more than 40 feet tall.

BUTTERCUPS

These bright yellow wildflowers are common in Rhode Island. They grow most often in cool areas during spring or early summer.

SCARLET PIMPERNELS

Scarlet pimpernels can be found growing on the cliffs of Newport. These plants have small, individual flowers that are bell-shaped before they open.

Rhode Island was the last state to adopt an official state flower. The state adopted the violet as its official flower in 1968.

Some farms in Rhode Island grow trees that bear cones, such as spruce, fir, and pine.

Rhode Island's "Christmas Greens" law protects certain trees and plants from being cut for Christmas holiday decorating. The law protects plants such as sea lavender and American holly.

Animals

The animal population of Rhode Island is dominated by small mammals. Rabbits, gray squirrels, woodchucks, raccoons, minks, beavers, and foxes can be found in the state's wilderness areas. White-tailed deer live on Prudence and Block islands and are the largest wild mammals found in Rhode Island.

A large variety of aquatic animals lives in the waters along the Atlantic coast. Cnidaria, a group of marine animals that have stinging **tentacles**, are common in the area. Cnidaria include jellyfish, corals, and sea anemones. Free-swimming jellyfish are saucer-shaped and are usually about the size of a human foot. Some types of jellyfish, however, can be as large as six feet in **diameter**.

RHODE ISLAND RED

The Rhode Island red became the state bird in 1954. A breed of chicken, the Rhode Island red has brownish red feathers and a single fleshy comb on its head.

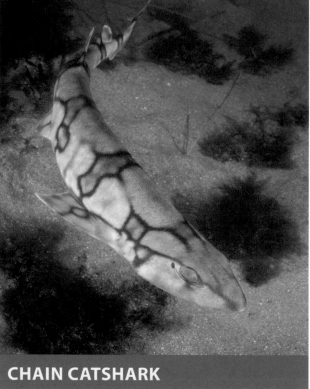

CHAIN CATSHARK

This small, spotted shark lives in the Atlantic Ocean from southern New England to Florida in the United States. These harmless animals feed in the deep water off the coast of Rhode Island.

FRILLED ANEMONE

Frilled anemones are about 1 foot tall. They have small tentacles that help the animal attach to rocks and shells during low and high tides.

RACCOON

The striped tail and masked face of a raccoon is a familiar sight in Rhode Island. These animals are most active during the night.

Rhode Island's state shell is the quahog. It was chosen on July 1, 1987. Local American Indians once used the shell of this clam as **currency**.

More than 300 species of birds have been identified in five national wildlife refuges in Rhode Island.

Although Rhode Island was once a whaling state, it is now trying to protect the northern right whale from extinction.

Blue sharks swim and feed in the open water far off the coast of Rhode Island. They can measure 11 feet long.

Tourism

Tourism is a vibrant and profitable industry in Rhode Island. Visitors have much to see and do in the Ocean State. The city of Newport has been called the Sailing Capital of the World because of the great opportunities for sailing in Narragansett Bay. **Yachts** have competed for the famed America's Cup just off the shore of Newport. Tourists can learn about the history of the America's Cup race at Bristol's Herreshoff Marine Museum, which includes the America's Cup Hall of Fame.

Newport has enough attractions to keep a tourist busy for weeks, on topics ranging from local history to architecture. Beginning in the late 1700s and especially in the late 1800s some of the nation's wealthiest citizens lived in beautiful homes in Newport. Today many of these homes are open to tourists.

ROGER WILLIAMS PARK ZOO

Opened in 1872, Roger Williams Park Zoo is one of the country's oldest zoos. More than 700,000 people visit the zoo in Providence each year to see Humboldt penguins, Dromedary camels, snow leopards, and a giant anteater exhibit.

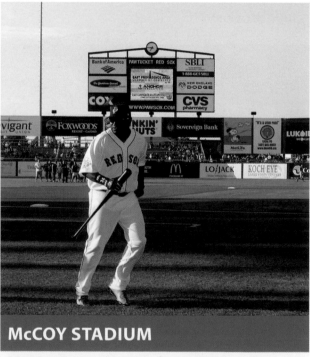

McCOY STADIUM

The Pawtucket Red Sox, or PawSox, play Triple-A Minor League baseball in McCoy Stadium. Recent upgrades to the stadium allow more than 10,000 fans to enjoy the game.

BLOCK ISLAND

Block Island covers almost 10 square miles. With its many freshwater ponds and public beaches, it is a popular tourist attraction in the summer. Visitors hike, sail, fish, and bicycle on the beautiful island.

THE BREAKERS

The Breakers in Newport is an opulent summer mansion open seasonally to visitors. It was built in 1895 in Italian Renaissance style for the Vanderbilt family. Today, the house is a National Historic Landmark.

Rhode Island's early colonial history is evident in every major city. There are restored colonial homes in North and South Kingstown, a restored colonial inn in Coventry, and military museums and armories throughout the state.

Hunter House in Newport was built in 1748 by the deputy governor of Rhode Island. It served as the headquarters of French naval commander Chevalier de Ternay during the American Revolution.

The Touro Synagogue in Newport is the nation's oldest **synagogue**. It was built in 1763. Today it is a National Historic Site.

Industry

I n the Ocean State, large fishing operations and independent fishers alike haul in flounder, butterfish, and cod near Galilee, the location of a fish-processing plant. The annual fish catch in Rhode Island is valued at more than $66 million. Lobsters and quahogs, or hardshell clams, are the most valuable catches.

Industries in Rhode Island
Value of Goods and Services in Millions of Dollars

Finance, insurance, and real estate together earn more than one quarter of Rhode Island's income. Why might industries such as these be so much larger than industries dependent on natural resources?

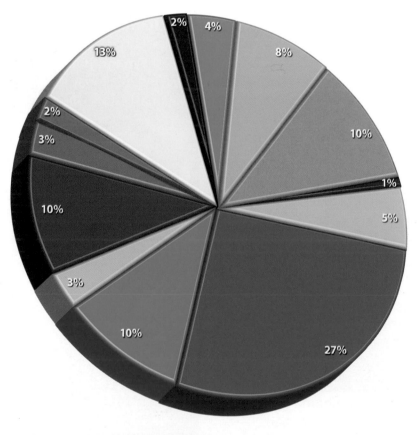

LEGEND

✳	Agriculture, Forestry, and Fishing	$83
✳	Mining	$37
■	Utilities	$872
■	Construction	$2,109
■	Manufacturing	$3,870
■	Wholesale and Retail Trade	$4,927
■	Transportation	$688
■	Media and Entertainment	$2,322
■	Finance, Insurance, and Real Estate	$13,015
■	Professional and Technical Services	$5,004
■	Education	$1,284
■	Health Care	$4,699
■	Hotels and Restaurants	$1,437
■	Other Services	$1,153
■	Government	$6,338

TOTAL **$47,838**

*Less than 1%. Percentages may not add to 100 because of rounding.

Agriculture, while less significant than it once was, remains important to Rhode Island's economy. Plant nurseries and turf harvesting are the chief agricultural activities. Greenhouse and nursery products account for about two-thirds of Rhode Island's agricultural income. These products include sod, ornamental trees, and shrubs. Dairy and poultry farms are also important, as are potato farms and apple orchards.

The U.S. Navy is the second largest employer in Rhode Island, after the state government. The Naval War College in Newport is one of the Navy's oldest institutions, having been in operation since 1884. Quonset Point Naval Air Station was a large base in Rhode Island during World War II, but the base was closed in 1974.

Milk is the second-largest source of agricultural income for Rhode Island.

I DIDN'T KNOW THAT!

By 1830 more than half of the workers at the Slater **textile** mill were children who worked for less than $1 a week. The practice of child labor is now illegal.

The first torpedo boat, *Stiletto*, was built in Bristol in 1887.

The Quonset hut, which was used as living quarters during World War II, was invented in Quonset, Rhode Island. The hut was made of metal and shaped like half a cylinder.

Goods and Services

Manufacturing was once the basis of Rhode Island's economy. In fact, following the American Revolution, the textile industry was Rhode Island's largest. Samuel Slater, recognized as the founder of the U.S. textile industry, opened his mill in Pawtucket. In recent years, however, the manufacturing of goods such as textiles, jewelry, and electrical equipment has fallen behind the service sector in terms of numbers of workers and amounts of income generated.

The leading industries in the service sector include private health care, law, and computer programming. With one of New England's largest banks headquartered in Rhode Island, finance is also important to the state. Citizens Bank employs thousands of people at its hundreds of branches.

The company that produces Nantucket Nectars bottled juice started as a small floating grocery store for boats. It now has a manufacturing and bottling plant in Warwick.

Tiffany is an internationally acclaimed jeweler, with stores throughout the world. It has a jewelry-manufacturing facility in Cumberland.

Some of Rhode Island's most important manufactured items are commonly found on necks and fingers and dangling from earlobes. As early as 1794 the state had made a name for itself in the jewelry industry. Nehemiah Dodge from Providence came up with a method, called plating, to cover inexpensive metals with precious metals. This **innovation** helped Rhode Island become the nation's jewelry-making center.

Rhode Island is still highly respected for its accomplished silversmiths and jewelers. Prominent manufacturers operating in Rhode Island include Colibri, Sardelli, Danecraft, and Tiffany & Co.

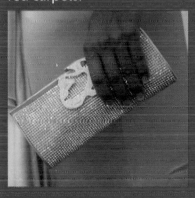

American Indians

The region now known as New England was inhabited by American Indians more than 10,000 years ago. Five separate groups lived in what is now Rhode Island. They were the Niantic, the Nipmuc, the Pequot, the Wampanoag, and the largest group, the Narragansett. All of them spoke related languages of the Algonquian language family. In Algonquian cultures, men fished and hunted while women planted, harvested, and prepared food. Women were also responsible for building the bark huts known as wigwams.

King Philip's War was named after Wampanoag chief Metacomet, or King Philip. In this 1675–1676 conflict, the American Indians of the region attempted and failed to push out the New England colonists.

In the early 1600s, approximately 7,000 Narragansett lived in the largest portion of what was to become Rhode Island. The area ranged from Warwick to South Kingstown and Exeter.

The Wampanoag were situated around the bay islands and the Providence and Warwick area. The Nipmuc, a smaller group, inhabited the northwest corner of Rhode Island. The Pequot lived along what is now the border with Connecticut, and the Niantic lived along the western coast.

Indian tribes in the Northeast made birchbark baskets for gathering food and storing personal items. Some were decorated with etched designs such as this basket with a deer and fox.

I DIDN'T KNOW THAT!

Before European settlement, the Pequot drove the Niantic out of Connecticut and then fought a major territorial war with the Narragansett in the 1630s.

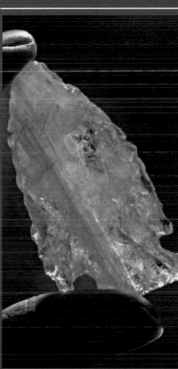

Indian arrowheads were uncovered on Block Island. They probably date back more than 2,000 years.

After King Philip's War, the Narragansett, the Niantic, and other Algonquian groups joined together to form a new American Indian community. They took the name Narragansett.

Explorers

European exploration of Rhode Island began about 500 years ago. The Portuguese sailor Miguel Corte-Real is thought to have traveled along the Rhode Island coast in the early 1500s. In 1524 Giovanni da Verrazzano came upon the area while searching for the **Northwest Passage** on behalf of King Francis I of France. Verrazzano explored Narragansett Bay and the island that later became known as Block Island. Some historians believe that he described the island as being approximately the same size as the island of Rhodes in the Mediterranean Sea. Later, settlers mistakenly thought that Verrazzano had been describing the island in Narragansett Bay that the American Indians called Aquidneck. They began calling that island Rhode Island.

In 1614 the Dutch explorer Adriaen Block visited Rhode Island while mapping the territory that Henry Hudson had explored earlier. Block may have been the first European to sail into Long Island Sound. He charted Long Island, showing it as a land mass separate from the island of Manhattan. He also came across Block Island and named it after himself.

Giovanni da Verrazzano was the first European to explore what is now New York harbor and Narragansett Bay. He later voyaged to Brazil but never returned.

Timeline of Settlement

Early Exploration

1524 Giovanni da Verrazzano sails to Narragansett Bay.

1614 Adriaen Block of Holland lands on an island in what is now called Block Island Sound and names the island after himself.

First Settlements

1636 Roger Smith establishes Providence Plantations.

1638–1643 The settlements of Portsmouth, Newport, and Warwick are founded.

British Rule and Conflict

1644 The English Parliament grants a charter recognizing the four Rhode Island settlements as a single colony.

1675–1676 Settlers defeat the American Indians in King Philip's War.

1775 British soldiers and American colonists battle at Lexington and Concord, in Massachusetts, marking the beginning of the American Revolution.

Independence and Statehood

1776 Rhode Island is the first colony to declare its independence from Britain.

1783 The American Revolution ends in the creation of the United States, with the separation of the American colonies from Great Britain.

1790 Rhode Island approves the new U.S. Constitution and becomes the 13th state in the Union.

1842 Thomas Dorr leads a rebellion in Rhode Island against laws limiting voting rights.

1843 Rhode Island passes a new state constitution with greater voting rights.

Early Settlers

Providence Plantations was the first permanent settlement in Rhode Island. It was established by Roger Williams in 1636. Williams, an English member of the clergy, and others had left the Massachusetts Bay Colony to pursue their religious beliefs.

Map of Settlements and Resources in Early Rhode Island

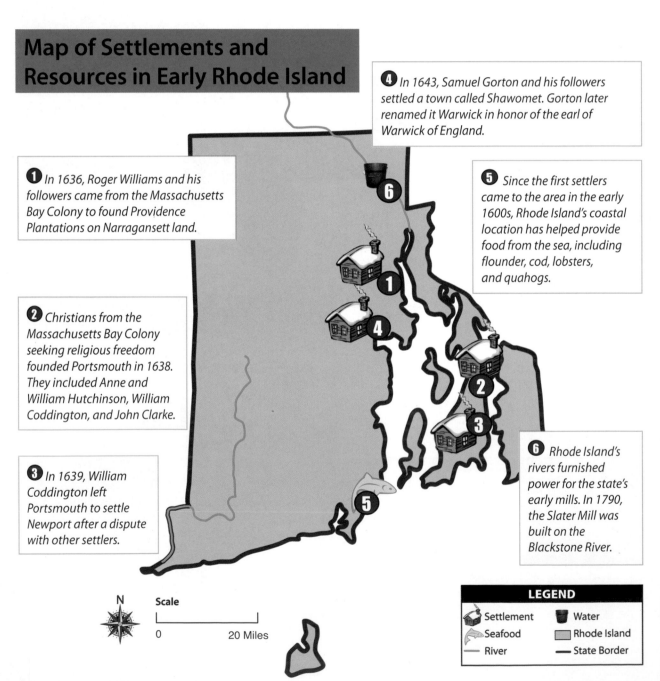

4 In 1643, Samuel Gorton and his followers settled a town called Shawomet. Gorton later renamed it Warwick in honor of the earl of Warwick of England.

1 In 1636, Roger Williams and his followers came from the Massachusetts Bay Colony to found Providence Plantations on Narragansett land.

5 Since the first settlers came to the area in the early 1600s, Rhode Island's coastal location has helped provide food from the sea, including flounder, cod, lobsters, and quahogs.

2 Christians from the Massachusetts Bay Colony seeking religious freedom founded Portsmouth in 1638. They included Anne and William Hutchinson, William Coddington, and John Clarke.

3 In 1639, William Coddington left Portsmouth to settle Newport after a dispute with other settlers.

6 Rhode Island's rivers furnished power for the state's early mills. In 1790, the Slater Mill was built on the Blackstone River.

N

Scale

0   20 Miles

LEGEND

Settlement		Water	
Seafood		Rhode Island	
River		State Border	

Other groups seeking religious freedom soon followed. Anne and William Hutchinson, William Coddington, and John Clarke founded Portsmouth in 1638. There they were free to practice their own form of Christianity.

In 1643, Samuel Gorton and others began a new settlement on Rhode Island. They left the Providence colony because it operated independently of English law. They felt that they could find freedom only while under the protection of the English. By the time the movement of Rhode Island's colonists began to slow down, there were four separate settlements in the area.

In 1644, Roger Williams pushed to unite the four Rhode Island settlements for protection from neighboring colonies. Later, in 1663, King Charles II granted a royal charter to Rhode Island and Providence Plantations, promising religious freedom, self-government, and independence. This charter remained law until 1843. It was the most liberal charter granted by England during the colonial period, and many of its guarantees served as the foundation for the rights and freedoms established in the U.S. Constitution.

Narragansett Indians gave shelter to Roger Williams after his banishment in 1635 from the Massachusetts Bay Colony. Williams founded Providence on land purchased from two Narragansett chiefs, Canonicus and Massasoit, in 1636.

Notable People

As the first colony to declare independence and the last of the original 13 to ratify the Constitution, Rhode Island has a reputation for independent thinkers. The Ocean State has been home to many political and military leaders, artists, and reformers who followed their strongly held beliefs and contributed to the development of their state and country.

ROGER WILLIAMS
(1603–1683)

Born in London, England, Williams came to America to seek greater freedom. He worked as a pastor in Boston in 1631 but was banned soon after for speaking out against forced worship. He fled to Narragansett Bay and founded Providence and later the colony of Rhode Island. Williams promoted liberty and democracy. He also believed in the rights of American Indians and learned the Narragansett language, writing *A Key into the Language of America* in 1643.

GILBERT STUART
(1755–1828)

Gilbert Stuart of Rhode Island painted celebrated portraits of U.S. presidents George Washington, John Adams, Thomas Jefferson, James Madison, and James Monroe. His historic painting of George Washington is on display at the Rhode Island State House in Providence. A reproduction of this work of art appears on the $1 bill.

OLIVER HAZARD PERRY (1785–1819)

Perry, born in South Kingston, was one of the nation's greatest naval commanders. He is often called the Hero of Lake Erie because of his victory at the Battle of Lake Erie in the War of 1812. About the British surrender he famously wrote, "We have met the enemy and they are ours." Perry died of yellow fever in 1819.

JULIA WARD HOWE (1819–1910)

Julia Ward Howe is perhaps best known for writing the patriotic poem "The Battle Hymn of the Republic," published in 1862. She was also a social reformer who worked for the rights of women and the end of slavery in the country. Born in New York City in 1819, Howe lived in Boston and South Portsmouth, where she died in 1910.

CLAIBORNE PELL (1918–2009)

Claiborne Pell represented the state of Rhode Island in the U.S. Senate for six terms, from 1961 until 1997. Largely through his efforts, the Federal Pell Grant Program, named for him, has provided financial aid to millions of college students since 1973. After retiring from the Senate, he was appointed U.S. delegate to the United Nations. Born in New York City in 1918, Pell died at the age of 90 in Newport.

Meredith Vieira (1953–) was born in Providence. She became coanchor of the NBC News morning program *The Today Show* in 2006. A former news correspondent for *60 Minutes*, Vieira is the winner of five Emmy Awards for her work.

Dee Dee Myers (1961–), born in Quonset Point, served as the White House press secretary for two years in the 1990s during the presidency of Bill Clinton. She was the first woman to hold the position.

Population

The population of Rhode Island is slightly more than 1 million. About one-sixth of Rhode Islanders live in Providence. The state is densely populated, with about 1,000 people per square mile. This is much higher than the national average of 87 people per square mile. Clearly, Rhode Islanders are quite "close" to their neighbors.

Rhode Island Population 1950–2010

Rhode Island's population grew more rapidly from 1950 to 1970 than it did over the following 40 years. What factors might account for these different rates of population growth?

Number of People

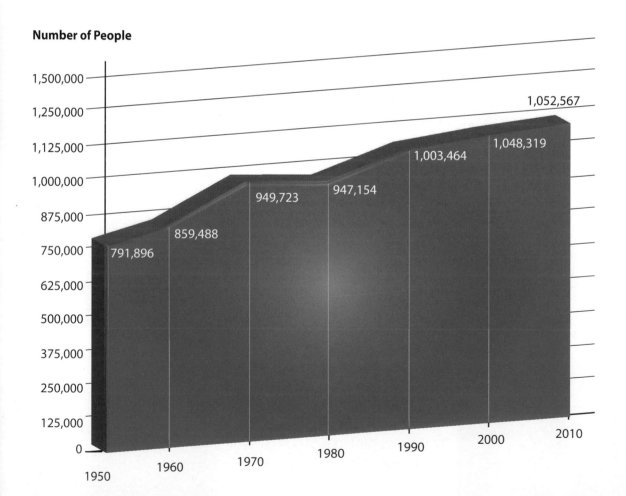

Year

The earliest European settlers in Rhode Island were English Protestants of various denominations. Because of its reputation for religious tolerance, Rhode Island also attracted Huguenots, or French Protestants, and Jews to settle during the colonial period.

Over the following centuries, waves of immigrants have added to Rhode Island's population. Irish immigrants settled in Providence, Pawtucket, and Newport in the 1820s, and French Canadians immigrated in the 1860s, during the Civil War. Germans, Swedes, and many people from Eastern Europe and Southern Europe arrived in the late 1800s and early 1900s.

With more than 170,000 residents, Providence is Rhode Island's largest city by population. It is the second-largest city in New England, after Boston.

Like the Capitol in Washington, D.C., the Rhode Island State House in Providence features a large central dome and two wings.

Politics and Government

Rhode Island's first constitution was the royal charter of 1663, which was granted by King Charles II. In 1842 state legislator Thomas Dorr led a rebellion in Rhode Island to protest laws that limited voting rights to men who owned a certain amount of property and to their eldest sons. The rebellion failed, but a new constitution with fewer voting restrictions was drawn up in the 1840s. The most recent state constitution was adopted in 1986.

There are three branches of state government in Rhode Island. They are the executive, legislative, and judicial branches. The governor serves as head of the executive branch. He or she is elected to a four-year term. The lieutenant governor, secretary of state, attorney general, and treasurer also serve four-year terms. The governor has **veto** power and the authority to appoint department heads. The legislative branch is the General Assembly, which is composed of 38 senators and 75 representatives. Rhode Island has a three-tier judiciary, with a Supreme Court serving as the last court of appeal.

The Rhode Island Independence Act, declaring freedom from Britain, was signed at the Old State House in Providence on May 4, 1776.

Cultural Groups

T he Narragansett people have a strong presence in Rhode Island. Although these American Indians sold their communal lands to the state in 1880, they worked to preserve their cultural traditions and established a registry to keep track of members. In 1934 the Narragansett adopted an elective form of government to select their chief and council. In 1977 they recovered 1,800 acres of their land from the U.S. government.

The traditional culture of the Narragansett is still strong today. For instance, the **powwow** is a time to come together in dance and song. The Narragansett gather every August to celebrate the annual Powwow and Green Corn Thanksgiving. Today a majority of the 2,400 descendants of the Narragansett who were registered in 1880 live in Washington and Providence counties. Smaller numbers are scattered throughout the rest of Rhode Island, as well as Connecticut and Massachusetts.

Various cultural groups contribute to Rhode Island's diversity. Students come to the state from all over the world, including Afghanistan, to earn degrees.

Although the percentage of African Americans in Rhode Island's population today is considerably smaller than the national average, the contributions of African Americans to the state are significant. During the American Revolution, blacks in New England, many of whom were slaves, supported the American colonies. While many states did not allow blacks to take up the fight for independence, Rhode Island had one of the only regiments that consisted mainly of black soldiers. Known as the First Rhode Island Regiment, these soldiers played an important role in the Battle of Rhode Island in 1778 by preventing the British from overtaking the Continental Army. After the American Revolution, some of these soldiers joined a new battle. Many became leaders in **abolition** movements throughout the North, working to end slavery in the United States.

Today the Rhode Island Black Heritage Society in Providence collects and preserves material relating to the role of African Americans in the state's history. Some photographs of the state's African American community leaders date back to about 1899.

Arts and Entertainment

For those interested in visual arts, Rhode Island has much to offer. The Newport International Film Festival, established in 1998, features independent and foreign films every June.

The Rhode Island School of Design, founded in 1877, is one of the foremost fine arts colleges in the nation. Its museum has more than 85,000 works of art in its collection. Works include early art from Greece, Rome, China, India, Egypt, and France as well as more modern masterpieces. Pendleton House, a wing of the museum, was built in 1906 to display Charles L. Pendleton's remarkable collection of furniture and decorative arts from the 1700s and 1800s. Pendleton House also exhibits the museum's large collection of American painting and sculpture, English ceramics, Chinese porcelain, and French wallpaper.

For several days each summer, musicians perform at an international celebration of jazz music at Fort Adams State Park. It is called the Newport Jazz Festival.

Audiences and students support several ballet organizations in Rhode Island. The State Ballet of Rhode Island, established in 1960, offers master classes, workshops, and summer camp to interested dancers.

A variety of musical styles are represented in the state. The Rhode Island Philharmonic Orchestra, the Providence Singers, and the annual Rhode Island Chamber Music Concerts offer some of the finest classical music performances in the state. The renowned Newport Jazz Festival, founded in 1954, is held annually.

There are many opportunities to enjoy ballet in Rhode Island. The State Ballet is Rhode Island's first company in residence. The Festival Ballet brings guest and touring companies to Rhode Island audiences from October to April. Rhode Island's Ballet Theater prepares young dancers for professional classical companies.

A majority of the state's dance and theater companies are based in Providence. One of them is the Trinity Repertory Company, which is known for its inventive and challenging performances. The dancers and choreographers at Groundwerx Dance Theater have been presenting traditional and modern dance performances since 1986.

I DIDN'T KNOW THAT!

The Flying Horse Carousel is the oldest carousel in the United States. It is located at Watch Hill.

George M. Cohan, a songwriter from the early 1900s, is known for composing the patriotic favorites "I'm a Yankee Doodle Dandy" and "You're a Grand Old Flag." Cohan was born in Providence in 1878.

Authors born in Rhode Island include H. P. Lovecraft, one of the first writers of modern horror novels, Galway Kinnell, a well-known poet, and Spalding Gray, who was also an actor.

The founding members of the rock group Talking Heads met while students at the Rhode Island School of Design.

Actress Debra Messing grew up in East Greenwich, outside of Providence. She won an Emmy Award in 2003 for her work on the sitcom *Will & Grace*.

Sports

Narragansett Bay is one of the largest saltwater recreational areas in New England. With more than 2,300 acres of beautiful parks on six islands, the state offers many residents a variety of outdoor activities. Sailing, biking, and hiking are just a few of the many activities enjoyed in Rhode Island. The state's small size makes bicycles ideal not only for recreation and exercise but also for transportation. Block Island is especially well suited to cycling, with spectacular scenery and winding roads.

Hikers can explore the varied terrain of Rhode Island. The southern and eastern areas of the state are relatively flat, with gently rolling hills. The northern and western sections, however, rise abruptly through dense woodlands. Many hikers head to the numerous islands, where they may encounter plants and animals that are found only in coastal areas.

Newport is widely known as the Sailing Capital of the World.

The International Tennis Hall of Fame hosts a professional competition in Newport each year with top players such as Andy Murray from Great Britain.

Newport was the site of the America's Cup Yacht Race from 1920 until 1983. The competition that determined the fastest racing **schooner** has been waged since 1851, when Great Britain's Royal Yacht Club offered to race its schooners against a challenger from the United States. The Americans won the race. A trophy was brought to the United States and named the America's Cup. It was put on display at the New York Yacht Club. In 1983 an Australian challenger won the America's Cup. This was the first time a challenger beat a U.S. yacht in 132 years.

Tennis lovers can find the oldest public grass courts in the United States at the International Tennis Hall of Fame. This museum is located in the Newport Casino. The Tennis Hall of Fame Museum features displays, artifacts, and exhibits that cover more than a century of tennis history.

I DIDN'T KNOW THAT!

Polo was played for the first time in the United States in 1876 near Newport.

The 132 years of successful defense of the America's Cup trophy by the New York Yacht Club is the longest record in sports history.

On the college level, Brown University's sports teams, the Brown Bears, Providence College's teams, the Providence Friars, are traditional rivals.

Paul Konerko, born in Providence, plays first base for the Chicago White Sox. He has been selected to the American League All-Star team several times.

National Averages Comparison

The United States is a federal republic, consisting of fifty states and the District of Columbia. Alaska and Hawai'i are the only non-contiguous, or non-touching, states in the nation. Today, the United States of America is the third-largest country in the world in population. The United States Census Bureau takes a census, or count of all the people, every ten years. It also regularly collects other kinds of data about the population and the economy. How does Rhode Island compare with the national average?

Comparison Chart

United States 2010 Census Data *	USA	Rhode Island
Admission to Union	NA	May 29, 1790
Land Area (in square miles)	3,537,438.44	1,044.93
Population Total	308,745,538	1,052,567
Population Density (people per square mile)	87.28	1007.31
Population Percentage Change (April 1, 2000, to April 1, 2010)	9.7%	0.4%
White Persons (percent)	72.4%	81.4%
Black Persons (percent)	12.6%	5.7%
American Indian and Alaska Native Persons (percent)	0.9%	0.6%
Asian Persons (percent)	4.8%	2.9%
Native Hawaiian and Other Pacific Islander Persons (percent)	0.2%	0.1%
Some Other Race (percent)	6.2%	6.0%
Persons Reporting Two or More Races (percent)	2.9%	3.3%
Persons of Hispanic or Latino Origin (percent)	16.3%	12.4%
Not of Hispanic or Latino Origin (percent)	83.7%	87.6%
Median Household Income	$52,029	$54,562
Percentage of People Age 25 or Over Who Have Graduated from High School	80.4%	78.0%

*All figures are based on the 2010 United States Census, with the exception of the last two items.

How to Improve My Community

S trong communities make strong states. Think about what features are important in your community. What do you value? Education? Health? Forests? Safety? Beautiful spaces? Government works to help citizens create ideal living conditions that are fair to all by providing services in communities. Consider what changes you could make in your community. How would they improve your state as a whole? Using this concept web as a guide, write a report that outlines the features you think are most important in your community and what improvements could be made. A strong state needs strong communities.

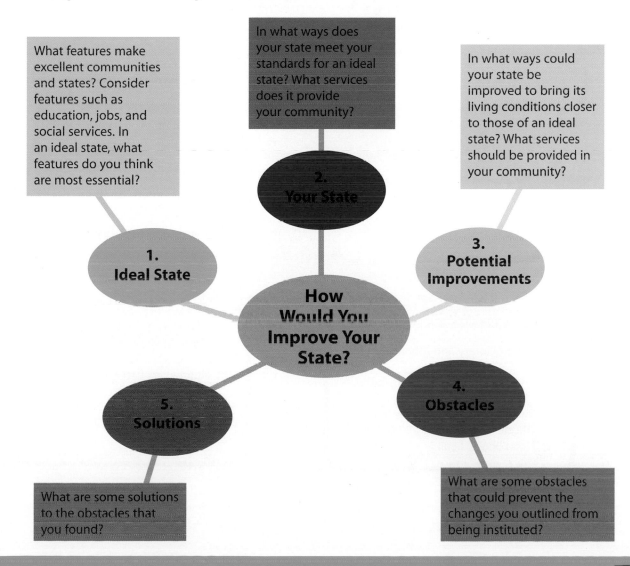

What features make excellent communities and states? Consider features such as education, jobs, and social services. In an ideal state, what features do you think are most essential?

In what ways does your state meet your standards for an ideal state? What services does it provide your community?

In what ways could your state be improved to bring its living conditions closer to those of an ideal state? What services should be provided in your community?

2. Your State

3. Potential Improvements

1. Ideal State

How Would You Improve Your State?

4. Obstacles

5. Solutions

What are some solutions to the obstacles that you found?

What are some obstacles that could prevent the changes you outlined from being instituted?

Exercise Your Mind!

Think about these questions and then use your research skills to find the answers and learn more fascinating facts about Rhode Island. A teacher, librarian, or parent may be able to help you locate the best sources to use in your research.

1 What does the statue at the top of the State Capitol in Providence depict?

2 Did Adriaen Block, the namesake of Block Island, discover the Northwest Passage?

3 True or False? The oldest schoolhouse in the United States is in Rhode Island.

4 Redwood Library and Athenaeum is:

a) The oldest library building in the United States
b) The library containing the largest Rhode Island historical collection
c) Not a library at all

5 True or False? Brown University has always gone by that name.

6 Roger Williams was the founder of what church?

7 What famous "summer cottage" is found in Newport?

8 Which of the following individuals was born in Rhode Island?

a) Filmmakers Peter and Bobby Farrelly
b) Sea captain Robert Gray
c) Inventor Stephen Wilcox
d) All of the above

Words to Know

abolition: the movement to put an end to slavery in the United States

currency: any form of money that is used as a means of exchange

diameter: a straight line that passes through the center of a circle and touches the outside of the circle at two points

eroded: worn away

hydroelectric: water-generated electric power

innovation: the creation of something new or different

Northwest Passage: a northern sea route thought to exist through North America from the Atlantic Ocean to the Pacific Ocean

powwow: a American Indian social gathering

ratify: to approve formally

schooner: a boat with a foremast and a mainmast

synagogue: a Jewish house of worship

tentacles: limblike features on certain animals, especially animals without a backbone, used for feeling, grasping, or moving

textile: woven products such as cloth, tapestries, or rugs

tolerated: accepted

veto: to officially disapprove and block, such as when a governor vetoes a bill passed by a legislature

yachts: light sailing vessels for racing

Index

Log on to www.av2books.com

AV² by Weigl brings you media enhanced books that support active learning. Go to www.av2books.com, and enter the special code found on page 2 of this book. You will gain access to enriched and enhanced content that supplements and complements this book. Content includes video, audio, web links, quizzes, a slide show, and activities.

Audio
Listen to sections of the book read aloud.

Video
Watch informative video clips.

Embedded Weblinks
Gain additional information for research.

Try This!
Complete activities and hands-on experiments.

WHAT'S ONLINE?

Try This!	Embedded Weblinks	Video	EXTRA FEATURES
Test your knowledge of the state in a mapping activity.	Discover more attractions in Rhode Island.	Watch a video introduction to Rhode Island.	**Audio** Listen to sections of the book read aloud.
Find out more about precipitation in your city.	Learn more about the history of the state.	Watch a video about the features of the state.	
Plan what attractions you would like to visit in the state.	Learn the full lyrics of the state song.		**Key Words** Study vocabulary, and complete a matching word activity.
Learn more about the early natural resources of the state.			
Write a biography about a notable resident of Rhode Island.			**Slide Show** View images and captions, and prepare a presentation.
Complete an educational census activity.			**Quizzes** Test your knowledge.

AV² was built to bridge the gap between print and digital. We encourage you to tell us what you like and what you want to see in the future.

Sign up to be an AV² Ambassador at www.av2books.com/ambassador.